Fact Finders®

A Primary Source History of

THE GOLD RUSH

by John Micklos, Jr.

Consultant: Richard Bell
Associate Professor of History
University of Maryland, College Park

CAPSTONE PRESS
a capstone imprint

Fact Finders Books are published by Capstone Press,
1710 Roe Crest Drive, North Mankato, Minnesota 56003
www.mycapstone.com

Library of Congress Cataloging-in-Publication Data
Cataloging-in-Publication Data is on file with the Library of Congress..
ISBN 978-1-4914-8486-9 (library binding)
ISBN 978-1-4914-8490-6 (paperback)
ISBN 978-1-4914-8494-4 (eBook PDF)

Editorial Credits
Brenda Haugen, editor; Sarah Bennett, designer; Wanda Winch, media researcher;
Katy LaVigne, production specialist

Photo Credits
Corbis: Bettmann, cover (bottom); Courtesy of Pamela Dixon, 20; Getty Images: Archive Photos, 21, Mark Kauffman, 4, Transcendental Graphics, 13; Granger, NYC, 7; Library of Congress: Prints and Photographs Division, 1 (bottom), 5, 17, 19; Newscom: Picture History, 25; North Wind Picture Archives, 9, 12, 27; Science Source, 15; Shutterstock: dade72, 29, Philip Bird LRPS CPAGB, 6; The Art Archives at Art Resource, N.Y., 23; Yale Collection of American Literature, Beinecke Rare Book and Manuscript Library, cover (top), 1 (top), 11

Printed in the United States 5426

TABLE OF CONTENTS

A NOTE ABOUT PRIMARY SOURCES

Primary sources are newspaper articles, photographs, speeches, or other documents that were created during an event. They are great ways to see how people spoke and felt during that time. You'll find primary sources from the time of the Gold Rush throughout this book. Within the text, primary source quotations are colored *brown* and set in italic type.

A GLEAM IN THE RIVER

The California Gold Rush started by accident. James Marshall was building a **mill** beside the American River in northern California in early 1848. On January 24, as Marshall gazed down into the water of the **millrace**, he saw something gleaming. *"My eye was caught by something shining in the bottom of the ditch,"* he later recalled. *"I reached my hand down and picked it up."* That gleaming something was a piece of gold. Soon Marshall spotted more gold. He showed it to some of his workers. They did not believe the gold was real.

Δ the original gold nugget James Marshall found

Marshall took the gold samples to John Sutter, who owned the mill property. Sutter tested them using simple tests from an encyclopedia. *"I declared this to be gold of the finest quality, of at least 23 carats,"* Sutter later wrote. The two men asked the workers at the mill site to keep the discovery a secret. Within weeks, however, word leaked out. Soon it spread to San Francisco, California. This small city of about 1,000 people was more than 100 miles (161 kilometers) away.

mill—a building with machines for turning wood, grain, or other materials into products

millrace—a channel that carries water to run a mill

Δ James Marshall at Sutter's Mill, next to the American River in northern California

People in the 19th century talked about "seeing the elephant" when describing an event of great excitement. In the 1840s few people in the United States had ever seen an elephant. There were not yet any zoos in the nation. Few people had a chance to attend a circus. The phrase became linked with the excitement of traveling to California in search of gold.

California was sparsely settled in the 1840s. Of the 170,000 people living in California, nearly all were American Indians. Marshall's discovery changed the course of history for California. In fact, it affected the entire United States.

Spain had claimed the land, which it called Alta California, ever since its sailors first explored it in the 1500s. For a long time the region remained largely unsettled. Father Junipero Serra founded the first of 21 Spanish **missions** in California in 1769. Population growth was slow. Mexico was the nearest source of settlers. At the time, Spain ruled Mexico. But few Mexicans wanted to move to Alta California. American Indian tribes roamed most of the land.

"We have seen Indians in immense numbers," Serra wrote. He added that the American Indians made *"a good* ***subsistence*** *on various seeds, and by fishing."* Soon their way of life would change forever.

A statue honoring Junipero Serra stands in Santa Barbara, California.

mission—a church or other place where missionaries live and work
subsistence—a living, at a basic level

Mexico gained independence from Spain in 1822. At the same time, Spain gave control of Alta California to Mexico. The land became a Mexican territory. More Mexican settlers began arriving.

Over time a few U.S. citizens began trickling in as well. Some came from the East Coast by ship, sailing around the tip of South America. Several opened businesses in small towns along the California coast. Others became ranchers. Trappers came from the Midwest looking for beaver furs.

By the 1840s tensions between the Mexicans and Americans living in Alta California had grown. Both groups wanted control of the territory. Some of the Americans sought independence from Mexico in 1846. The rebels flew a flag with an image of a grizzly bear. Their movement became known as the Bear Flag Revolt.

▽ one of the original flags of the Bear Flag Revolt

As that small conflict was unfolding, the U.S. declared a broader war on Mexico. The war began over ownership of Texas, but U.S. President James Polk also hoped to gain control of California. He had tried to buy the land from Mexico, but Mexico refused to sell it. By July 1846 the American flag replaced the bear flag. Pioneer John Bidwell noted that the bear flag *"had no importance to begin with, none whatever when the Stars and Stripes went up."*

Although the U.S. had gained control of California, the territory still legally belonged to Mexico. But the outcome of the Mexican-American War would soon change that. U.S. troops captured the Mexican capital of Mexico City in 1847. Soon the fighting was over. The two nations began working on a peace treaty.

Meanwhile, California businessmen such as Sutter built stores and mills to meet the needs of settlers. The discovery of gold in 1848 sped up the region's growth. **Migration** and settlement that would normally take decades instead took place within just a few years.

Shortly after gold was discovered, the peace treaty ending the war between the U.S. and Mexico was signed. In the treaty Mexico gave vast territories to the U.S. for $15 million. These lands included present-day California. At the time neither the Mexican nor U.S. governments knew just how valuable this land would prove to be.

migration—movement of people

U.S. gains after Mexican-American War

GOLD FEVER

News about the discovery of gold spread slowly at first. There were no telephones or email or even regular mail service. But businessman Sam Brannan wanted to spread news of the discovery. He owned a small store not far from the goldfields. He thought that if more people knew about the gold, his store would get more business.

Brannan bought pickaxes, shovels, pans, and other items miners would need. In May 1848 he traveled to San Francisco. Brannan went through the streets carrying a bottle filled with gold dust. *"Gold! Gold! Gold from the American River!"* he shouted. Within a few days most of San Francisco's population had left to search for gold. Brannan made a fortune selling mining supplies.

But Brannan wanted even more attention, and he used a newspaper he owned to get it. He printed a special issue that included an announcement of the gold discovery. *"From all accounts the mine is immensely rich,"* the article stated, *"and already, we learn, the gold from it is collected at random and without any trouble."* Brannan sent 2,000 copies of the special issue east by mule. He hoped to bring thousands of other miners to his store. The newspapers reached Missouri in July. From there, the news continued to slowly spread east.

EL DORADO

OF THE

UNITED STATES OF AMERICA.

THE DISCOVERY

OF

INEXHAUSTIBLE GOLD MINES

IN

CALIFORNIA.

Tremendous Excitement among the Americans.

The Extensive Preparations

TO

MIGRATE TO THE GOLD REGION.

&c. &c. &c.

The great discovery of gold, in dust, scales and lumps, of quicksilver, platina, cinnabar, &c., &c., on the shores of the Pacific, has thrown the American people into a state of the wildest excitement. The intelligence from California, that gold can be picked up in lumps, weighing six or seven ounces, and scooped up in tin pans at the rate of a pound of the pure dust a scoop, whilst rich supplies of quicksilver, platina, &c., &c., are so plentiful as to be entirely neglected for the more precious metal, has set the inhabitants of this great republic almost crazy. "Ho! for California," is the cry every where. "Ho! for California," heads columns of advertisements in all the newspapers of the day. In a word, "Ho! for California" startles many a delirious one in his dreams at night.

All the intelligence from the gold region, and all the information relating thereto, is therefore sought for with the greatest avidity; and it is with the view of satisfying the public on this point, that we publish THE CALIFORNIA HERALD.

We shall endeavor, in the following account, to give as connected a narrative of the discovery of California, of the gold mines, of the excitement produced in the settled States, the preparations making to emigrate thither, &c., &c., &c., as our space will permit; and we illustrate the whole with a splendid and most accurate "MAP OF THE GOLD AND QUICKSILVER DISTRICT IN CALIFORNIA." This map gives the latest topographical survey of the mineral region, since the discovery of the rich gold mines, and was drawn by an officer of the American Army, on the spot. It was sent to us through the medium of Lieut. Loeser, of the Third Artillery, who came across the Isthmus, and reached Washington a week or two ago, as bearer of the important gold despatch of Gov. Mason. It can, therefore, be relied on as authentic in every detail.

THE DISCOVERY OF THE MINES.

Their Richness—The Effect in California,

&c., &c., &c.

Official Account of the Gold Region.

QUARTERMASTER'S OFFICE, SAN FRANCISCO, CALIFORNIA, Sept. 18, 1848.

SIR.—In compliance with an intimation in my monthly report of June 30, I proceed to give you a hasty account of California, as it is seen under the influence of the gold excitement now prevailing throughout the country. I shall precede my remarks upon the mines by a few observations upon the situation of the country prior to their discovery.

Up to the time the American flag was raised in California, by Commodore Sloat, in July, 1846, the country may be said to have slumbered on from its first settlement, without enterprise or activity on the part of its inhabitants. Constitutionally indolent in their habits, the climate was admirably adapted to develope and perpetuate the worst forms of slothfulness and improvidence among the occupants of the soil. The people were too much the victims of these vices to become even shepherds in the true sense of the word; and they lived without either milk, butter, or cheese, although surrounded by thousands of milch cows; and scarcely an attempt was made to call out the agricultural virtues of the soil. A little wheat and corn, and a few beans, pumpkins, and melons, satisfied the moderate wants of those who had never known the comforts to be derived from industry, and the grand staple of subsistence with all classes was the flesh of their cattle. The listlessness and apathy of this kind of life clung to the whole native population, and when the United States flag was raised here, the country could boast of no improvements, either public or private, except what the moderate wants of a warm latitude rendered imperatively necessary.

There were many Americans and foreigners in the country prior to the change of flags; but no regular emigration had taken place, and the unsettled condition of politics, and constant revolutions, prevented anything like the systematic enterprise which might otherwise have been expected from citizens of Anglo-American origin. The herds of cattle which covered the ranchos were slaughtered for their hides and tallow, to be exchanged for merchandise as before, and the people continued to cherish their indolence as much as in former days; but the change of flags brought a corresponding revolution in the various occupations of life. After the first call for volunteers was answered, and foreigners residing in the country were at leisure to enter upon the improvement of their property, all became activity. Confidence was inspired by the introduction of American authority, and all believed that they were virtually upon United States soil. Crowds came thronging in from the mountains, the forests, and the ocean; of rough exterior, but of indubitable Anglo-American origin, to seek their fortunes in a new country, under their own flag. Things soon assumed a better aspect, and both agricultural and mechanical improvements were going forward rapidly under new auspices. Farmers were introducing the agriculture and horticulture of their own country upon California soil, and mechanical labor knew no respite from its toils. The interminable clatter of the hammer and the saw was heard in every quarter; and frequently the mechanic, in his eagerness to succeed, did not recollect to "divide the Sunday from the week." Many little villages sprang up, as if by magic, in various parts of the country; and all promised fair for an indefinite continuance of every kind of improvement.

But a change came over the face of affairs. In the latter part of February, 1848, a mechanic, named James W. Marshall, was employed in building a sawmill for John A. Sutter, Esq., on the south branch of a river known in California as the American Fork, some fifty miles from New Helvetia, or Sutter's Fort. On Fremont's map this river is called "Rio de los Americanos." It is the stream by which Captain Fremont descended into the valley of the Sacramento river, by a perilous march, in the winter and spring of 1843. While employed in cutting a mill-race or canal for this improvement, Mr. Marshall discovered the pieces of gold as they glistened in the sunlight at the bottom of the sluice. Pieces of considerable size were taken from the water, and in a few days gold to the amount of one hundred and fifty dollars was removed in this manner. The laborers on the works, mostly Mormons, soon became satisfied of its precious nature, and the news spread rapidly about the country. Examinations were prosecuted at other points along the stream, and almost everywhere with success. Reports of a most marvellous nature soon reached the coast, touching these mines. Their apparent extravagance created incredulity, and the public attention was not fully called to the subject until gold dust or grain gold was brought into the market in considerable quantities for sale. Doubt soon became belief, and a change almost magical in its nature pervaded the whole population. Lawyers, doctors, clergymen, farmers, mechanics, merchants, sailors, and soldiers, left their legitimate occupation, to embark in a business where fortunes were to be made in a few weeks. Villages and districts, where all had been bustle, industry, and improvement, were soon left without male population. Mechanics, merchants, and magistrates, were alike off to the mines, and all kinds of useful occupation, except gold digging, were apparently at an end. In most cases the crops were remarkably good; but they are generally lost for want of laborers to secure them. In some parts of the country hundreds of acres of fine wheat will rot in the fields, from the impossibility of getting laborers. Vessels are left swinging idly at their anchors, while both captains and crews are at the mines; and the most essential private and public improvements are arrested in their progress. The wages of clerks have advanced at least two hundred per cent., and those of common laborers at least four or five hundred. At the time the excitement broke out, I was repairing the United States bark "Anita." The workmen were receiving \$3 per day, and lived on board the vessel. They struck for higher wages, and one man finally left and forfeited all his previous earnings, rather than to continue at work a few days more at \$5 per day. Common sailors demanded \$100 per month for work on schooners in the bay. Freight from this port to Sutter's is from \$2 to \$4 per barrel. The distance is little more than one hundred miles. Common four-ox wagons are hired at \$50 per day. In one case I have known a negro cook to be employed at \$25 per day for his professional services among the pots and kettles in the gold regions.

This was the condition of things about three months

Δ A newspaper shared the story that gold was found in California.

The first gold seekers from outside California arrived in the spring and summer of 1848. They came from Oregon, Hawaii, and Mexico. Soon others seeking their fortunes came from Europe, China, Australia, and South America. News had reached them on boats traveling across the oceans.

By fall 1848 news of the gold discovery reached the eastern United States. Some people learned about it from Brannan's newspaper. Others heard reports from some of the early miners who had struck gold. Newspapers ran huge articles about the gold rush. The *Baltimore Sun* said: *"Rich Gold Fields Have Been Discovered in California!"* The *New York Herald* ran a story that said, *"The real **El Dorado** has at length been discovered."*

El Dorado—a mythical city of amazing wealth

At first people found these stories hard to believe. But in December 1848, President James Polk said that the discoveries were likely real. *"Recent discoveries render it probable that these mines are more extensive and valuable than was anticipated,"* he said.

Many people took the dangerous overland journey west to California. Most expeditions left from towns along the Missouri River. The travelers crossed prairies, mountains, and deserts. Some faced attacks from **hostile** American Indian tribes. The tribes were angry about the number of people **trespassing** on their lands. About 9 out of 10 of the people heading to California in search of gold were men. A few brave women also traveled with their husbands. *"I thought where he could go I could, and where I went I could take my two little toddling babies,"* wrote Luzena Wilson.

Δ Wagons and stagecoaches crossed the Sierra Nevadas into California during the Gold Rush.

hostile—unfriendly or angry
trespass—to go on another's property without permission

CRITICAL THINKING

Why do you think so few women and children traveled to California as part of the Gold Rush?

Tens of thousands of gold seekers journeyed to California in 1849. Many called themselves '49ers. Some sailed from New York and other East Coast cities by going around the tip of South America. That trip took several months. Others saved time by crossing Panama on foot. In Panama miners faced dense jungles, bugs, and disease. *"We were here attacked by one of the most ravenous swarms of musquitos it was ever my lot to encounter,"* said John M. Letts.

Gold seekers came from many parts of the world, but they all had one thing in common. They hoped to make a fortune in California.

◁ A promotional card for the clipper ship *Richard S. Ely* sailing to San Francisco and the California goldfields was printed in New York.

LIFE IN THE GOLDFIELDS

Some people who reached the California goldfields in 1848 and early 1849 became rich. Mexican-born Antonio Franco Coronel found abundant gold. In just three days, he dug up more than 8 pounds (3.6 kilograms) of the precious metal. Miner S. Shufelt arrived in the goldfields in 1849 from New York. He found gold in many places. *"It is found along the banks of the streams & in the beds of the same, & in almost every little ravine putting into the streams,"* Shufelt wrote.

Not everyone had such success. By the time most of the '49ers arrived, the easy pickings were gone. Mining gold was hard work. Most miners did **placer mining**. Each miner worked in one small area called a claim. Miners shoveled gravel, dirt, or mud into a metal pan shaped like a pie pan. Then they swirled water around the pan. The water carried the lighter dirt, sand, and gravel over the edge of the pan. The gold was heavier. It remained at the bottom.

A '49er panned for gold along the American River in California in 1850. ▷

placer mining—mining done in a stream bed, often in a single area

Life was hard for most miners. They spent at least six days a week sifting dozens of pans of dirt each day hoping to find bits of gold. It was backbreaking work. Miners lived crammed together in groups of tents or poorly built cabins. Many spent Sundays in bars and gambling halls.

Some miners described how tough their lives were. Brothers Ethan Allen and Hosea Grosh left Pennsylvania in early 1849. They hoped to find gold in California. They sent letters home telling how hard they worked and how little gold they found. In November 1849 Allen wrote: *"We are still 'dwellers in a tent' and such a tent! Medium horsehair cloth would yield better protection.... In good spirits despite of mud and rain."*

Miners paid high prices for everyday items. A single egg could cost $25 in today's money. Coffee sometimes sold for what today would be more than $100 per pound. And a pair of boots might cost $2,500 or more in today's money. Even miners who found small amounts of gold had to spend most of their earnings on food and clothing.

Miners from other countries had an even more difficult time. They often faced **discrimination**. Many were chased away from their claims with threats of violence. Antonio Franco Coronel had lived in California for many years. Still, other miners forced him to leave a rich claim because he was a foreigner.

CRITICAL THINKING

What are some reasons people might have discriminated against miners from outside of the United States?

There was little formal justice in the mining camps. Most miners lived by informal rules, such as the Miner's Ten Commandments. One said: *"Thou shalt have no other claim than one."* Another stated: *"Thou shalt not steal a pick, or a shovel, or a pan from thy fellow miner...."* Some miners ignored these rules. Theft and even murder were common. As crime increased, some mining camps formed Committees of Vigilance. These groups carried out informal trials when crimes were committed. People found guilty were often **lynched**.

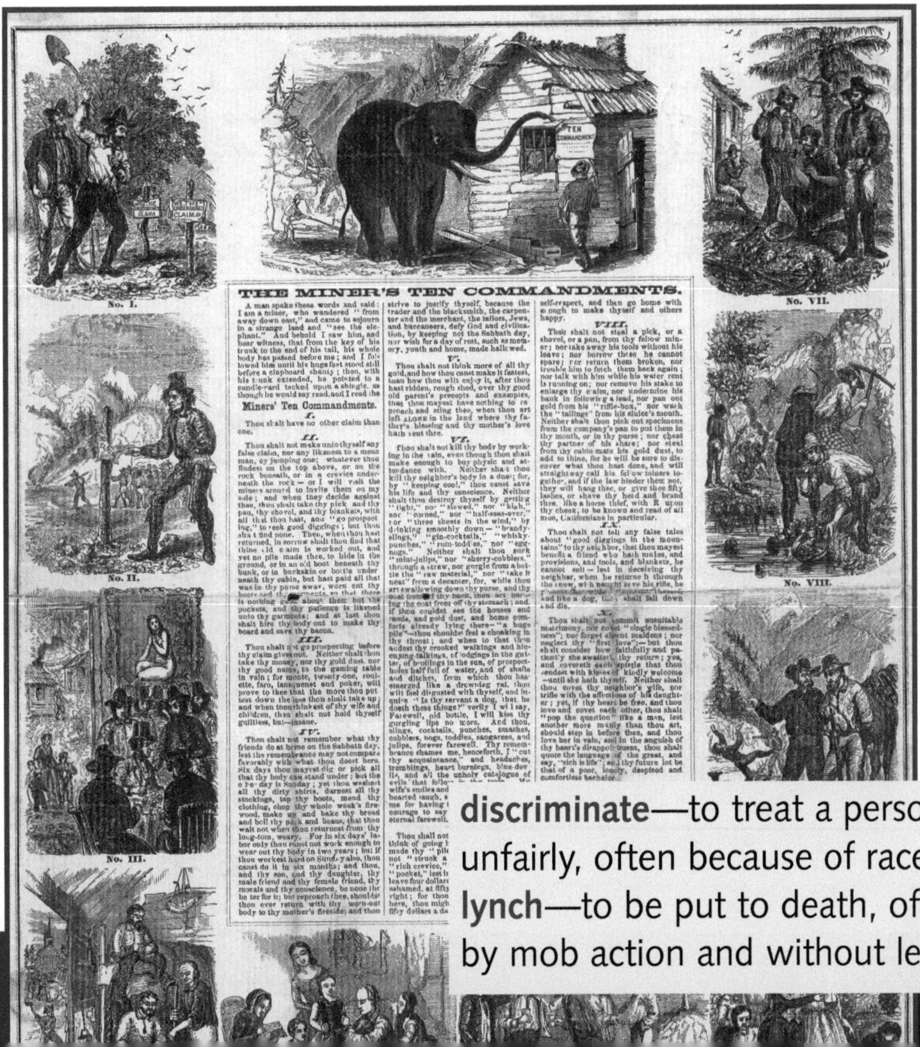

THE MINER'S TEN COMMANDMENTS.

A man spake these words and said: I am a miner, who wandered "from away down east," and came to sojourn in a strange land and "see the elephant." And behold I saw him, and bear witness, that from the key of his trunk to the end of his tail, his whole body has passed before me; and I followed him until his huge feet stood still before a clapboard shanty; then, with his trunk extended, he pointed to a candle-card tacked upon a shingle, as though he would say read, and I read the

Miners' Ten Commandments.

I.

Thou shalt have no other claim than one.

II.

Thou shalt not make unto thyself any false claim, nor any likeness to a mean man, by jumping one; whatever thou findest on the top above, or on the rock beneath, or in a crevice underneath the rock — or I will visit the miners around to invite them on my side; and when they decide against thee, thou shalt take thy pick and thy pan, thy shovel, and thy blankets, with all that thou hast, and "go prospecting," to seek good diggings; but thou shalt find none. Then, when thou hast returned, in sorrow shalt thou find that thine old claim is worked out, and yet no pile made thee, to hide in the ground, or in an old boot beneath thy bunk, or in buckskin or bottle underneath thy cabin, but hast paid all that was in thy purse away, worn out thy boots and thy garments, so that there is nothing good about them but the pockets, and thy patience is likened unto thy garments; and at last thou shalt hire thy body out to make thy board and save thy bacon.

III.

Thou shalt not go prospecting before thy claim gives out. Neither shalt thou take thy money, nor thy gold dust, nor thy good name, to the gaming table in vain; for monte, twenty-one, roulette, faro, lansquenet and poker, will prove to thee that the more thou puttest down the less thou shalt take up; and when thou thinkest of thy wife and children, thou shalt not hold thyself guiltless, but—insane.

IV.

Thou shalt not remember what thy friends do at home on the Sabbath day, lest the remembrance may not compare favorably with what thou doest here. Six days thou mayest dig or pick all that thy body can stand under; but the other day is Sunday; yet thou washest all thy dirty shirts, darnest all thy stockings, tap thy boots, mend thy clothing, chop thy whole week's firewood, make up and bake thy bread and boil thy pork and beans, that thou wait not when thou returnest from thy long-tom, weary. For in six days' labor only thou canst not work enough to wear out thy body in two years; but if thou workest hard on Sunday also, thou canst do it in six months; and thou, and thy son, and thy daughter, thy male friend and thy female friend, thy morals and thy conscience, be none the better for it; but reproach thee, shouldst thou ever return with thy worn-out body to thy mother's fireside; and thou strive to justify thyself, because the trader and the blacksmith, the carpenter and the merchant, the tailors, Jews, and buccaneers, defy God and civilization, by keeping not the Sabbath day, nor wish for a day of rest, such as memory, youth and home, made hallowed.

V.

Thou shalt not think more of all thy gold, and how thou canst make it fastest, than how thou wilt enjoy it, after thou hast ridden, rough shod, over thy good old parent's precepts and examples, that thou mayest have nothing to reproach and sting thee, when thou art left ALONE in the land where thy father's blessing and thy mother's love hath sent thee.

VI.

Thou shalt not kill thy body by working in the rain, even though thou shalt make enough to buy physic and attendance with. Neither shalt thou kill thy neighbor's body in a duel; for, by "keeping cool," thou canst save his life and thy conscience. Neither shalt thou destroy thyself by getting "tight," nor "slewed," nor "high," nor "corned," nor "half-seas-over," nor "three sheets in the wind," by drinking smoothly down — "brandy-slings," "gin-cocktails," "whisky-punches," "rum-toddies," nor "egg-nogs." Neither shalt thou suck "mint-juleps," nor "sherry-cobblers," through a straw, nor gurgle from a bottle the "raw material," nor "take it neat" from a decanter, for, while thou art swallowing down thy purse, and thy coat from off thy back, thou art burning the coat from off thy stomach; and, if thou couldst see the houses and lands, and gold dust, and home comforts already lying there—"a huge pile"—thou shouldst feel a choking in thy throat; and when to that thou addest thy crooked walkings and hiccuping-talkings, of lodgings in the gutter, of broilings in the sun, of prospect-holes half full of water, and of shafts and ditches, from which thou hast emerged like a drowning rat, thou wilt feel disgusted with thyself, and inquire "Is thy servant a dog, that he doeth these things?" verily I will say, Farewell, old bottle, I will kiss thy gurgling lips no more. And thou, slings, cocktails, punches, smashes, cobblers, nogs, toddies, sangarees, and julips, forever farewell. Thy remembrance shames me, henceforth, I "cut thy acquaintance," and headaches, tremblings, heart burnings, blue-devils, and all the unholy catalogue of evils that follo[illegible] wife's smiles and hearted laugh, [illegible] me for having [illegible] courage to say eternal farewell.

Thou shall not think of going h[illegible] made thy "pil[illegible] not "struck a [illegible] "rich crevice," [illegible] "pocket," lest i[illegible] leave four dollar[illegible] ashamed, at fifty [illegible] right; for thou [illegible] here, thou migh[illegible] fifty dollars a da[illegible] self-respect, and then go home with enough to make thyself and others happy.

VIII.

Thou shalt not steal a pick, or a shovel, or a pan, from thy fellow miner; nor take away his tools without his leave; nor borrow those he cannot spare; nor return them broken, nor trouble him to fetch them back again; nor talk with him while his water rent is running on; nor remove his stake to enlarge thy claim, nor undermine his bank in following a lead, nor pan out gold from his "riffle-box," nor wash the "tailings" from his sluice's mouth. Neither shalt thou pick out specimens from the company's pan to put them in thy mouth, or in thy purse; nor cheat thy partner of his share; nor steal from thy cabin-mate his gold dust, to add to thine, for he will be sure to discover what thou hast done, and will straightway call his fellow miners together, and if the law hinder them not, they will hang thee, or give thee fifty lashes, or shave thy head and brand thee, like a horse thief, with R upon thy cheek, to be known and read of all men, Californians in particular.

IX.

Thou shalt not tell any false tales about "good diggings in the mountains" to thy neighbor, that thou mayest benefit a friend who hath mules, and provisions, and tools, and blankets, he cannot sell — lest in deceiving thy neighbor, when he returneth through the snow, with naught save his rifle, he [illegible] and like a dog, thou shalt fall down and die.

X.

Thou shalt not commit unsuitable matrimony, nor covet "single blessedness"; nor forget absent maidens; nor neglect thy "first love";—but thou shalt consider how faithfully and patiently she awaiteth thy return; yea, and covereth each epistle that thou sendest with kisses of kindly welcome —until she hath thyself. Neither shalt thou covet thy neighbor's wife, nor trifle with the affections of his daughter; yet, if thy heart be free, and thou love and covet each other, thou shalt "pop the question" like a man, lest another more manly than thou art, should step in before thee, and thou love her in vain, and in the anguish of thy heart's disappointment, thou shalt quote the language of the great, and say, "sich is life"; and thy future lot be that of a poor, lonely, despised and comfortless bachelor.

◁ The Miner's Ten Commandments were the only rules many miners lived by in their camps.

discriminate—to treat a person or group unfairly, often because of race or religion

lynch—to be put to death, often by hanging, by mob action and without legal authority

THE VEINS RUN DRY

Most of the easy-to-reach gold was gone by 1851. At that point some miners quit working their own claims. Instead they worked for wages for large mining companies. Some companies dug deep mines. Others blasted jets of water at streambeds. They hoped to uncover gold buried beneath the rocks. Miners **extracted** about $81 million of gold in 1852. Then the figures declined. In all, more than 750,000 pounds (340,194 kg) of gold were mined during the Gold Rush.

A few miners found wealth. Most found only disappointment. Hiram Pierce of Troy, New York, left behind a wife and seven children in search of riches. After two years in California, he sold his shovel for $2. He headed home with nothing to show for all his work.

"I have made an honest effort," Pierce wrote. *"I will no longer sacrifice all that is dear on earth or worth living for, for the hope of gain."*

CRITICAL THINKING

How do you think the families of miners managed during the long time apart?

extract—

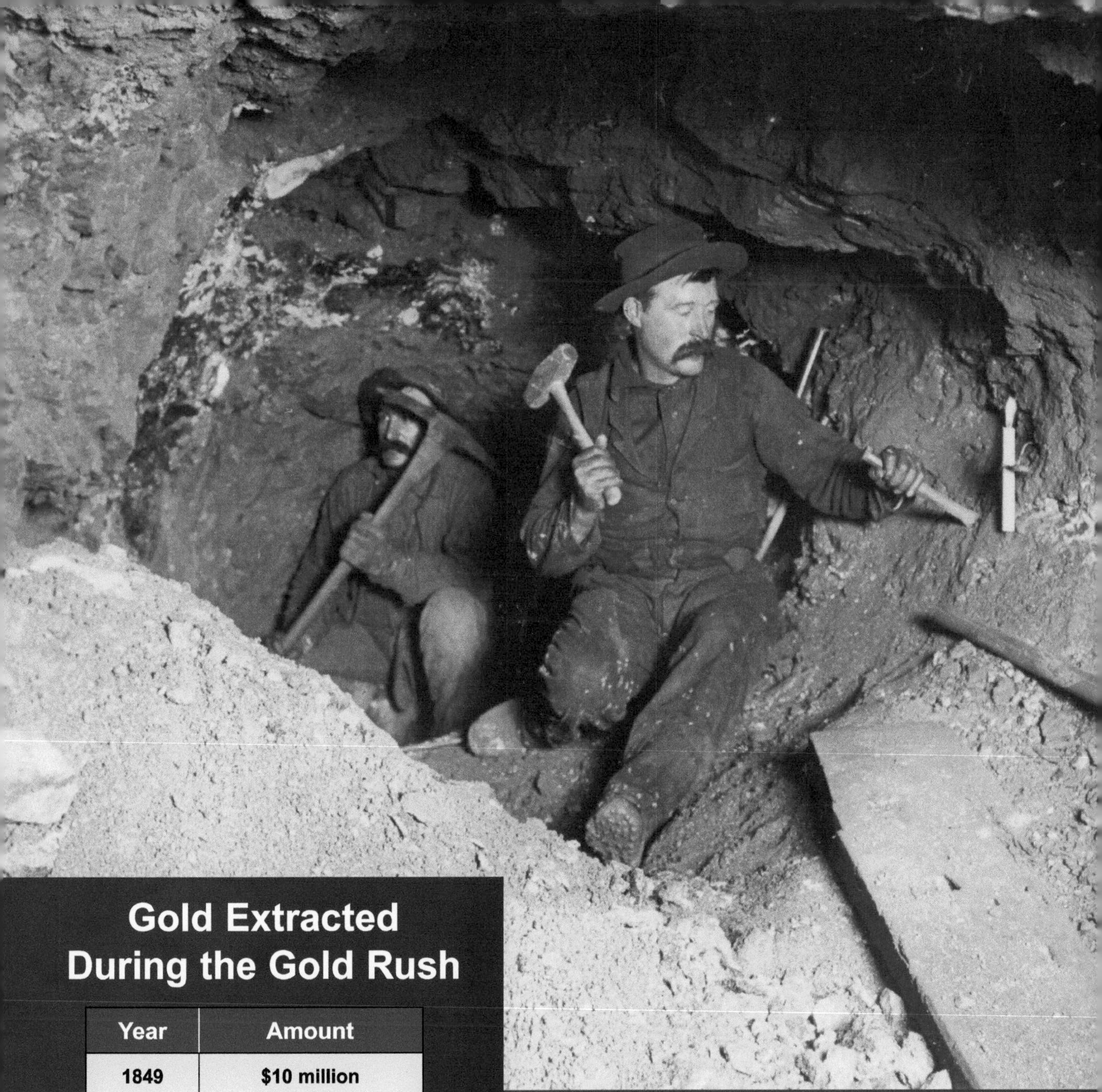

Gold Extracted During the Gold Rush

Year	Amount
1849	$10 million
1850	$41 million
1851	$75 million
1852	$81 million
1857	$45 million
1860–1880	$170 million

Δ Miners sometimes worked deep underground to find gold.

Charles H. Harvey left his wife in Ohio in 1852 in search of gold. He wrote in his diary about giving up his unsuccessful mining efforts. He ended up working on a farm, chopping wood, and doing other odd jobs just to survive. *"Have been searching for work but found none, Dull times,"* Harvey wrote. *"Do not know what to do … almost out of money."* Like Pierce, he returned home without the riches he had hoped to find.

A few miners made a fortune finding gold. Those are the stories that most people heard about. But most of the wealth from the Gold Rush went to business people who served the needs of miners and settlers.

For instance, most miners longed for home-cooked food and a decent place to sleep. After one miner offered Luzena Wilson $10 for some homemade biscuits, she and her husband decided to build a small hotel in a mining camp. She served meals to hungry miners from a table she built herself.

Δ Luzena Wilson

"With my own hands I chopped stakes, drove them into the ground, and set up my table," Wilson later wrote. She used two boards as the tabletop. Wilson named her hotel El Dorado. For her the Gold Rush did bring at least modest wealth.

Levi Strauss began selling dry goods in San Francisco in 1853. Among the items he sold were clothes for miners. Years later he partnered with Jacob Davis to make special pants held together with rivets to make them stronger. Farmers, cowboys, and others flocked to buy these sturdy denim pants. Because they were dyed blue, the pants later earned the nickname "blue jeans." Strauss became famous for his overalls, but he got his start in business during the Gold Rush.

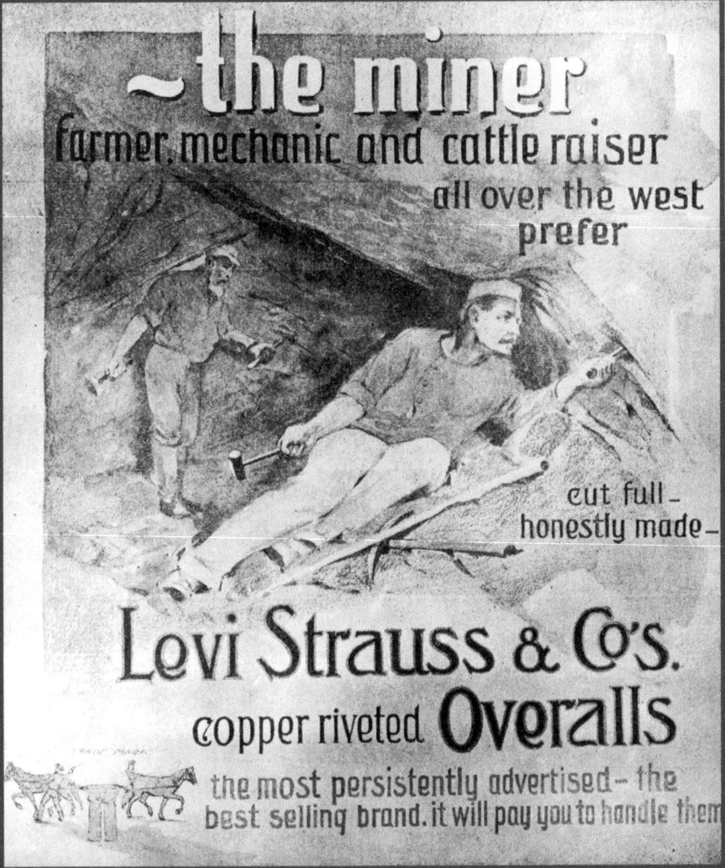

an ad for overalls, showing the tough garments that were popular with miners

CALIFORNIA KEEPS GROWING

Some '49ers settled in the rapidly growing city of San Francisco. Others moved to towns that were springing up near the goldfields. San Francisco had fewer than 1,000 residents in early 1848. By the end of 1850, it had 30,000.

California became the nation's 31st state on September 9, 1850. *"Our State is a marvel to ourselves, and a miracle to the rest of the world,"* Nathaniel Bennett said. Bennett was one of the first justices to serve on California's Supreme Court.

Even after the Gold Rush wound down in the 1850s, California's growth continued. Some miners returned home after the Gold Rush. But in many other cases, families moved to California to join them. They built new lives as settlers in California.

∇ San Francisco in 1849, the year the California Gold Rush began

Population Growth of San Francisco

Year	Population
1846	200
1847	459
1848	850
1849	25,000
1860	56,802
1870	149,473
1900	342,782
1950	775,357
1980	678,974
2000	776,733
2010	805,235
2015	837,442

Immigrants came pouring in to California from other countries. They hoped to find a better life. Thousands of Chinese immigrants settled in San Francisco. Many opened restaurants or laundries. At first nearly all of the Chinese immigrants were men. Of the nearly 12,000 Chinese living in California in 1852, only seven were women. Over time, Chinese families came as well. The state's population grew rapidly.

Not everyone benefitted from California's growth. The American Indians who had lived there for hundreds of years suffered greatly. First gold seekers and later settlers pushed the American Indians off their lands. Within 20 years of the end of the Gold Rush, about 120,000 American Indians—about three out of four—had died. Most died from starvation and disease.

"And this gold strike brought thousands of people from every place known to man into our traditional territory," said April Moore, a present-day educator and member of the Nisenan Maidu tribe. The Nisenan Maidu tribe lived in the area around Sutter's Mill. *"They overused the area and created drought and created starvation for themselves, and along with them for the* ***indigenous*** *peoples."*

immigrant—a person who moves from one country to live permanently in another country

Δ Many miners, such as those on the right, came to California from China.

The treaty with Mexico that had given California to the United States described how American Indians should be treated. *"Special care shall then be taken not to place its Indian occupants under the necessity of seeking new homes,"* the treaty stated. That promise was not fulfilled.

Likewise, the two men most responsible for starting the California Gold Rush failed to profit from it. Neither James Marshall nor John Sutter found much gold after that first day. Both failed in most of their business ventures as well. As they aged, they felt bitter that wealth had passed them by. Sutter wished gold had been discovered a few years later after his mill was more established. Then, he believed, he *"would have been the richest citizen on the Pacific shore. [But] instead of being rich, I am ruined."* He believed that the way the Gold Rush had developed prevented him from making his mill and other ventures successful.

CRITICAL THINKING

Do you think the timing of the Gold Rush was to blame for Sutter's failures? Why or why not?

Δ Originally from Switzerland, John Sutter settled in California before the Gold Rush.

For many people, however, California lived up to its nickname as "The Golden State." Some people took advantage of the state's rich soil. They became successful farmers. Others launched businesses to serve the needs of the state's rapidly growing population. Later the state would become the center of the world's movie industry.

Decades after the Gold Rush ended, people continued to flock to California. They still believed the state offered a chance for fame and fortune—or at least a better life than they had before. As a result, California has become the nation's most populated state.

Even without the Gold Rush, people would have discovered the many benefits California had to offer. Still, the accidental discovery of the "gleam in the river" made a huge difference. It set off a chain of events that changed the state's—and the nation's—history.

Δ modern day San Francisco

CRITICAL THINKING

How might the development of California have been different if gold had not been discovered?

SELECTED BIBLIOGRAPHY

Brands, H.W. *The Age of Gold: The California Gold Rush and the New American Dream.* New York: Doubleday, 2002.

"The Gold Rush of 1849." Online by History.com. www.history.com/topics/gold-rush-of-1849

Jackson, Donald Dale. *Gold Dust.* Lincoln, Neb.: University of Nebraska Press, 1982.

Johnson, Susan Lee. *Roaring Camp: The Social World of the California Gold Rush.* New York: W.W. Norton, 2000.

Lapp, Rudolph M. *Blacks in Gold Rush California.* New Haven, Conn.: Yale University Press, 1977.

Levy, JoAnn. *They Saw the Elephant: Women in the California Gold Rush.* Hamden, Conn.: Archon Books, 1990.

Marks, Paula Mitchell. *Precious Dust: The American Gold Rush Era: 1848–1900.* New York: W. Morrow, 1994.

"Paths to Empire: Constitutional Convention and Statehood." Online by the University of California at Berkeley. http://bancroft.berkeley.edu/Exhibits/Looking/pathstoempire.html

Sutter, Gen. John A. "The Discovery of Gold in California." Online by The Virtual Museum of the City of San Francisco. www.sfmuseum.net/hist2/gold.html

"Vigilante Justice, 1851." Online by EyeWitness to History.com. www.eyewitnesstohistory.com/vigilante.htm

GLOSSARY

discriminate (dis-KRI-muh-nayt)—to treat a person or group unfairly, often because of race or religion

El Dorado (EL doh-RAH-doh)—a mythical city of amazing wealth

extract (ek-STRAKT)—to remove

hostile (HOSS-tuhl)—unfriendly or angry

immigrant (IM-uh-gruhnt)—a person who moves from one country to live permanently in another country

indigenous (in-DI-juh-nuhss)—native to a place

lynch (LINCH)—to be put to death, often by hanging, by mob action and without legal authority

migration (mye-GRAY-shuhn)—movement of people from one area to another

mill (MIL)—a building with machines for turning wood, grain, or other materials into products

millrace (MIL-rayss)—a channel that carries water to run a mill

mission (MISH-uhn)—a church or other place where missionaries live and work

placer mining (PLAY-ser MY-ning)—mining done in a stream bed, often in a single area

subsistence (suhb-SIS-tuhns)—a living at a basic level

trespass (TRESS-pass)—to go on another's property without permission

INTERNET SITES

FactHound offers a safe, fun way to find Internet sites related to this book. All of the sites on FactHound have been researched by our staff.

Here's all you do:

Visit *www.facthound.com*

Type in this code: 9781491484869

INDEX